Francis Frith's
WORCESTERSHIRE

PHOTOGRAPHIC MEMORIES

Francis Frith's
WORCESTERSHIRE

◆

John Bainbridge

FRITH
BOOK CO

First published in the United Kingdom in 2000 by
Frith Book Company Ltd

Text and Design copyright © Frith Book Company Ltd
Photographs copyright © The Francis Frith Collection

British Library Cataloguing in Publication Data

Worcestershire
John Bainbridge
ISBN 1-85937-152-3

Frith Book Company Ltd
Frith's Barn, Teffont,
Salisbury, Wiltshire SP3 5QP
Tel: +44 (0) 1722 716 376
Email: info@frithbook.co.uk
www.frithbook.co.uk

Printed and bound in Great Britain

Front Cover: **Worcester, The Cross 1923** 73755

Contents

Francis Frith: Victorian Pioneer   7

Frith's Archive - A Unique Legacy   10

Worcestershire - An Introduction   12

Worcestershire - A–Z   17

Index   115

Free Mounted Print Voucher   *119*

FRANCIS FRITH: *Victorian Pioneer*

FRANCIS FRITH, Victorian founder of the world-famous photographic archive, was a complex and fascinating man. A devout Quaker and a highly successful Victorian businessman, he was both philosophic by nature and pioneering in outlook.

By 1855 Francis Frith had already established a wholesale grocery business in Liverpool, and sold it for the astonishing sum of £200,000, which is the equivalent today of over £15,000,000. Now a multi-millionaire, he was able to indulge his passion for travel. As a child he had pored over travel books written by early explorers, and his fancy and imagination had been stirred by family holidays to the sublime mountain regions of Wales and Scotland. 'What a land of spirit-stirring and enriching scenes and places!' he had written. He was to return to these scenes of grandeur in later years to 'recapture the thousands of vivid and tender memories', but with a different purpose. Now in his thirties, and captivated by the new science of photography, Frith set out on a series of pioneering journeys to the Nile regions that occupied him from 1856 until 1860.

INTRIGUE AND ADVENTURE

He took with him on his travels a specially-designed wicker carriage that acted as both dark-room and sleeping chamber. These far-flung journeys were packed with intrigue and adventure. In his life story, written when he was sixty-three, Frith tells of being held captive by bandits, and of fighting 'an awful midnight battle to the very point of surrender with a deadly pack of hungry, wild dogs'. Sporting flowing Arab costume, Frith arrived at Akaba by camel seventy years before Lawrence, where he encountered 'desert princes and rival sheikhs, blazing with jewel-hilted swords'.

During these extraordinary adventures he was assiduously exploring the desert regions bordering the Nile and patiently recording the antiquities and peoples with his camera. He was the first photographer to venture beyond the sixth cataract. Africa was still the mysterious 'Dark Continent', and Stanley and Livingstone's historic meeting was a decade into the future. The conditions for picture taking confound belief. He laboured for hours in his wicker dark-room in the sweltering heat of the desert, while the volatile chemicals fizzed dangerously in their trays. Often he was forced to work in remote tombs and caves where conditions were cooler. Back in London he exhibited his photographs and was 'rapturously cheered' by members of the Royal Society. His reputation as a photographer was made overnight. An eminent modern historian has likened their impact on the population of the time to that on our own generation of the first photographs taken on the surface of the moon.

VENTURE OF A LIFE-TIME

Characteristically, Frith quickly spotted the opportunity to create a new business as a specialist publisher of photographs. He lived in an era of immense and sometimes violent change. For the poor in the early part of Victoria's reign work was a drudge and the hours long, and people had precious little free time to enjoy themselves.

Most had no transport other than a cart or gig at their disposal, and had not travelled far beyond the boundaries of their own town or village. However, by the 1870s, the railways had threaded their way across the country, and Bank Holidays and half-day Saturdays had been made obligatory by Act of Parliament. All of a sudden the ordinary working man and his family were able to enjoy days out and see a little more of the world.

With characteristic business acumen, Francis Frith foresaw that these new tourists would enjoy having souvenirs to commemorate their days out. In 1860 he married Mary Ann Rosling and set out with the intention of photographing every city, town and village in Britain. For the next thirty years he travelled the country by train and by pony and trap, producing fine photographs of seaside resorts and beauty spots that were keenly bought by millions of Victorians. These prints were painstakingly pasted into family albums and pored over during the dark nights of winter, rekindling precious memories of summer excursions.

THE RISE OF FRITH & CO

Frith's studio was soon supplying retail shops all over the country. To meet the demand he gathered about him a small team of photographers, and published the work of independent artist-photographers of the calibre of Roger Fenton and Francis Bedford. In order to gain some understanding of the scale of Frith's business one only has to look at the catalogue issued by Frith & Co in 1886: it

runs to some 670 pages, listing not only many thousands of views of the British Isles but also many photographs of most European countries, and China, Japan, the USA and Canada – note the sample page shown above from the hand-written *Frith & Co* ledgers detailing pictures taken. By 1890 Frith had created the greatest specialist photographic publishing company in the world, with over 2,000 outlets – more than the combined number that Boots and WH Smith have today! The picture on the right shows the *Frith & Co* display board at Ingleton in the Yorkshire Dales. Beautifully constructed with mahogany frame and gilt inserts, it could display up to a dozen local scenes.

POSTCARD BONANZA

The ever-popular holiday postcard we know today took many years to develop. In 1870 the Post Office issued the first plain cards, with a pre-printed stamp on one face. In 1894 they allowed other publishers' cards to be sent through the mail with an attached adhesive halfpenny stamp. Demand grew rapidly, and in 1895 a new size of postcard

was permitted called the court card, but there was little room for illustration. In 1899, a year after Frith's death, a new card measuring 5.5 x 3.5 inches became the standard format, but it was not until 1902 that the divided back came into being, with address and message on one face and a full-size illustration on the other. *Frith & Co* were in the vanguard of postcard development, and Frith's sons Eustace and Cyril continued their father's monumental task, expanding the number of views offered to the public and recording more and more places in Britain, as the coasts and countryside were opened up to mass travel.

Francis Frith died in 1898 at his villa in Cannes, his great project still growing. The archive he created continued in business for another seventy years. By 1970 it contained over a third of a million pictures of 7,000 cities, towns and villages. The massive photographic record Frith has left to us stands as a living monument to a special and very remarkable man.

Frith's Archive: *A Unique Legacy*

FRANCIS FRITH'S legacy to us today is of immense significance and value, for the magnificent archive of evocative photographs he created provides a unique record of change in 7,000 cities, towns and villages throughout Britain over a century and more. Frith and his fellow studio photographers revisited locations many times down the years to update their views, compiling for us an enthralling and colourful pageant of British life and character.

We tend to think of Frith's sepia views of Britain as nostalgic, for most of us use them to conjure up memories of places in our own lives with which we have family associations. It often makes us forget that to Francis Frith they were records of daily life as it was actually being lived in the cities, towns and villages of his day. The Victorian age was one of great and often bewildering change for ordinary people, and though the pictures evoke an impression of slower times, life was as busy and hectic as it is today.

We are fortunate that Frith was a photographer of the people, dedicated to recording the minutiae of everyday life. For it is this sheer wealth of visual data, the painstaking chronicle of changes in dress, transport, street layouts, buildings, housing, engineering and landscape that captivates us so much today. His remarkable images offer us a powerful link with the past and with the lives of our ancestors.

TODAY'S TECHNOLOGY

Computers have now made it possible for Frith's many thousands of images to be accessed almost instantly. In the Frith archive today, each photograph is carefully 'digitised' then stored on a CD Rom. Frith archivists can locate a single photograph amongst thousands within seconds. Views can be catalogued and sorted under a variety of categories of place and content to the immediate benefit of researchers. Inexpensive reference prints can be created for them at the touch of a mouse button, and a wide range of books and other printed materials assembled and published for a wider, more general readership - in the next twelve months over a hundred Frith local history titles will be published! The day-to-

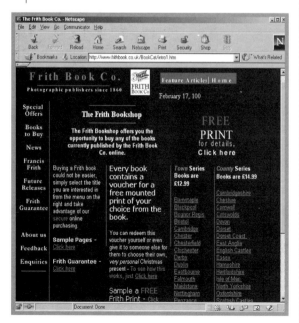

See Frith at www. frithbook.co.uk

day workings of the archive are very different from how they were in Francis Frith's time: imagine the herculean task of sorting through eleven tons of glass negatives as Frith had to do to locate a particular sequence of pictures! Yet the archive still prides itself on maintaining the same high standards of excellence laid down by Francis Frith, including the painstaking cataloguing and indexing of every view.

It is curious to reflect on how the internet now allows researchers in America and elsewhere greater instant access to the archive than Frith himself ever enjoyed. Many thousands of individual views can be called up on screen within seconds on one of the Frith internet sites, enabling people living continents away to revisit the streets of their ancestral home town, or view places in Britain where they have enjoyed holidays. Many overseas researchers welcome the chance to view special theme selections, such as transport, sports, costume and ancient monuments.

We are certain that Francis Frith would have heartily approved of these modern developments, for he himself was always working at the very limits of Victorian photographic technology.

THE VALUE OF THE ARCHIVE TODAY

Because of the benefits brought by the computer, Frith's images are increasingly studied by social historians, by researchers into genealogy and ancestory, by architects, town planners, and by teachers and schoolchildren involved in local history projects. In addition, the archive offers every one of us a unique opportunity to examine the places where we and our families have lived and worked down the years. Immensely successful in Frith's own era, the archive is now, a century and more on, entering a new phase of popularity.

THE PAST IN TUNE WITH THE FUTURE

Historians consider the Francis Frith Collection to be of prime national importance. It is the only archive of its kind remaining in private ownership and has been valued at a million pounds. However, this figure is now rapidly increasing as digital technology enables more and more people around the world to enjoy its benefits.

Francis Frith's archive is now housed in an historic timber barn in the beautiful village of Teffont in Wiltshire. Its founder would not recognize the archive office as it is today. In place of the many thousands of dusty boxes containing glass plate negatives and an all-pervading odour of photographic chemicals, there are now ranks of computer screens. He would be amazed to watch his images travelling round the world at unimaginable speeds through network and internet lines.

The archive's future is both bright and exciting. Francis Frith, with his unshakeable belief in making photographs available to the greatest number of people, would undoubtedly approve of what is being done today with his lifetime's work. His photographs, depicting our shared past, are now bringing pleasure and enlightenment to millions around the world a century and more after his death.

WORCESTERSHIRE - *An Introduction*

APART FROM THOSE who know it well, the average traveller most often regards Worcestershire only from the speeding lanes of the M5 motorway, which cuts so cruelly across the heart of this enchanting county. Even so, they may be vaguely aware that the long line of hills rising dramatically to the west are the Malverns, and that the lovely rounded summit to the east is that very same Bredon Hill so celebrated in poetry, song and painting.

But for the people who live and work in the surrounding countryside, with its busy towns and pretty villages, this is a place to be cherished, rich in historical importance and immortalised in English culture. Worcestershire is also a playground for thousands of visitors from the industrial conurbations of the Midlands, who seek out its rivers and peaceful countryside as an escape from the workaday world. Discerning tourists from farther afield have long known of the joys of Worcestershire, seeking out the delights of the Malverns and the north-west

Cotswolds, the Cathedral City of Worcester and the boating rivers of the Stour and Severn. But sometimes you are left with the impression that not enough people in Britain appreciate quite how beautiful Worcestershire is, and how much it deserves protection from the ravages of the modern age.

Worcestershire is the county of Sir Edward Elgar, perhaps the nation's favourite composer. Elgar certainly found much inspiration in his native landscape, and it is hard to walk across the Malverns without his melodies singing through your mind. He was born at The Firs in Upper Broadheath in 1857, and attended school in Worcester. His greatest happiness and source of inspiration was to spend a day walking across Worcestershire's hilltops or water meadows, plucking music out of the air. Elgar lived for many years at Great Malvern, working on some of his greatest compositions whilst he was there. It is a magical experience for anyone who loves Elgar's music to seek out the church porch at Longdon Marsh and sit there for a while, as the composer did during a violent thunderstorm when the music for 'The Apostles' first came into his head, or to walk the high beacons of the Malvern range with the notes of the 'Enigma Variations' or 'The Dream of Gerontius' humming through your soul. For it was probably on just such a walk that Elgar first envisaged these great works of English music.

Bredon Hill is immortalised in the works of the poet A E Housman; despite being the acclaimed and much-quoted author of 'A Shropshire Lad', he was actually born at Fockbury, just outside Bromsgrove, living most of his life in that latter town. 'In Summertime on Bredon' and the other poems in the cycle capture the pastoral traditions of this lovely countryside to perfection; they were written at a time when many of the photographs in this book were being taken. It is not too difficult to wander over Bredon Hill and the villages nearby and feel the rural idyll portrayed in Housman's verse:

Here of a Sunday morning
My love and I would lie,
And see the coloured counties,
And hear the larks so high
About us in the sky.

Bredon Hill is a kind of barrier between the plains of Worcestershire and the Cotswolds; all of this land was part of the ancient kingdom of Mercia even before King Offa's time.

Worcester itself is not just the capital of this entrancing area, but as good a centre as any for its exploration. The city is as much loved

Cropthorne, The Village 1901 47321

by those who know it as the countryside around. The unfortunate King John may have had his faults, but he is redeemed somewhat by his love of Worcester, a place he included in virtually every Royal Progress he undertook. It was at his own request that he was buried before the High Altar of Worcester Cathedral.

The great joy in the photographs which follow is that the Frith photographers were careful to include in their collection not just the popular visitor spots, such as Bredon, Worcester and the Malverns, but many of the less tourist-haunted towns and villages as well. These were captured for ever at a time before the area was over-dominated by the motor car, and when buildings could be observed without the distractions of street furniture.

A journey through Worcestershire takes us not only in the footsteps of many famous men and women, but also in the steps of those forgotten souls who lived fascinating lives on their own terms and lie buried in the local churchyards. They too left their marks on this landscape; some of the more recent of them are pictured herein, going about their existences just as the good people of Worcestershire have done for generations in this ancient county.

HISTORIC WORCESTERSHIRE

When the poet William Langland walked the Malverns seven centuries ago and looked across the plains, river valleys and distant hilltops of Worcestershire, he was already admiring a landscape that was old in time. Yet in many ways the most dramatic events of the county's history were yet to come.

In prehistoric times, much of what are now the pasturelands of Worcestershire would have been covered with trees; much of the lowest ground was impenetrable except to the hardiest and most determined of travellers. The highways of the day were the ridge paths across the high ground, where flint tools and weapons are still sometimes found today by the walkers who follow in our ancestors' footsteps. It is likely that the great rivers of Worcestershire - the Severn, Stour, Teme and Avon - were used as water highways as well, much as they are today. It was in the Neolithic age that man began to hack away at Worcestershire's forests, and the process would have been well advanced by Langland's time.

Certainly, many of the pastures we know today would have been under cultivation, for is not Langland's poem entitled 'The Vision Concerning Piers the Plowman'? Feudal agriculture was at its height in the 1300s, and the villages we see in the following photographs were already in existence, with the street patterns and churches much as we know them now. Worcester's Cathedral soared over its city as did other great abbeys and religious houses. The Cathedral remains, but many of the other Christian establishments that would have been so familiar to Langland have gone for ever - demolished in the calculated acts of vandalism which followed Henry VIII's Dissolution of the monasteries. The Reformation also led to changes in the landscape thereabouts, for the Church had owned much of the countryside. This was hastily grabbed by noble and commoner alike when the power of the Church was reduced.

Langland's Worcestershire was a relatively peaceful place in comparison to what had gone before and what was yet to come, though the war between Henry III and Simon de Montfort and the Barons of England, which culminated in the murderous Battle of Evesham, was probably still talked about in the evening firelight. In 1401 the Welsh patriot Owain Glyndwr invaded, for the was hurriedly put in a state of defence for Charles I; an early conflict took place at Powick Bridge between Fiennes' Roundheads and Charles' nephew Prince Rupert. After the inconclusive battle at Edgehill, Worcester was abandoned by the Parliamentary troops who had occupied it, though the Roundhead General Sir William Waller made valiant attempts to retake the city. In the four years

Worcester, The Cross 1896 38931

borders of Wales and the Marches beyond were disputed territory for several centuries. Glyndwr sacked and burnt Worcester itself, but sensibly retired back to the mountains and passes of Wales before he could be brought to battle on Woodbury Hill.

Two hundred and fifty years later, the whole of Worcestershire became an extended battleground for Royalists and Parliamentarians in the English Civil War. When the war broke out in 1642, Worcester

that followed, until the final defeat of the Royalists at Naseby, there was a considerable amount of skirmishing up and down Worcestershire. Many villages could probably tell a tale of conflict.

In August 1651, Charles II marched down from Scotland in an attempt to oust his late father's enemies and reclaim the throne. On 3 September Charles' exhausted army awaited the arrival of Oliver Cromwell's New Model Army, which had crossed the Severn and

Teme by boat-bridges. Bitter hand-to-hand fighting took place in and around Worcester, and Charles' forces were gradually overwhelmed. Charles was fortunate to escape, for tradition alleges that there was just the distance of one house between himself and his pursuers across the heart of the city. An epic journey to the South Coast and long years of exile were to follow before Charles II's Restoration in 1660.

Much of the troop movements of these and the earlier conflicts which shaped England's history can still be followed on the ground; though as we drive along today's roads, it is difficult to appreciate the difficulties of march and counter-march along the muddy tracks which passed for highways in those days, or how difficult it was to cross broad rivers on bridges that had been 'slighted' to create a watery obstacle course for the frustration of your enemies.

The history of Worcestershire is there to be seen and interpreted in the county's landscape and buildings, whether church or cottage, castle or medieval bridge. The scenes captured by the Frith photographers are, of course, as important a part of our social history as the desperate deeds of the Civil War.

Captured for ever are the village streets before they were surrendered to the motor car; and so are the broad hilltops and rolling meadows that seem to disappear a little more each year as urbanisation grips England. Here are the local shops which people relied upon for their weekly provisions in earlier times. Most of all, here are the people of Worcestershire just being themselves, living their lives in this most attractive and historical county. They are, perhaps, not so different from the medieval residents portrayed so tellingly by William Langland.

Worcester, The Cross 1899 44010

ABBERLEY, THE TOWER 1911 64057
Abberley Hill and Woodbury Hill rise to about a thousand feet. This 161 feet high clock tower caps the latter, and is known locally as Jones's Folly. The tower was built in the latter half of the 19th century, complete with a carillon of bells designed to play forty-two tunes.

ABBERLEY, FROM THE CARILLON TOWER 1911 64056

Abberley Hall is part of an estate dating back to the Norman Conquest, when King William gave it to his supporter Todeni. The present house, seen here, goes back only to 1845. The original family home burnt down in a fierce blaze on Christmas Day 1845.

ABBERLEY, GENERAL VIEW C1965 A255041

During the reign of Henry IV, the King's army marched around these hills seeking to bring the Welsh patriot Owain Glyndwr to battle. Peaceful Abberley might have become one of the notable battlefields of England and changed the course of history, had not the elusive Glyndwr slipped back across the Welsh Marches.

BELBROUGHTON, HARTLE LANE c1965 B418004

Belbroughton is happily situated just south of the Clent Hills. There is a great deal of attractive Georgian architecture, and a church dating back to the 12th century, with a beautifully decorated 15th-century font and handsome Carolean pulpit and reading desk.

BELBROUGHTON, HIGH STREET c1965 B418007

Belbroughton parish contains parts of the three Domesday Manors of Belne, Brocton and Farfield. Car ownership in rural Worcestershire had become widespread by this time, though many, such as those queuing outside this shop, still relied on the local bus.

BEWDLEY
Load Street 1931 84620
Leland was most impressed with Bewdley: 'The towne
is set on the syd of a hill, so coningly that a man
cannot wishe to set a towne better...at the rysnge of
the sunne from este the whole towne glittereth, being
all of new building, as it wer of gold'.

BEWDLEY, LOAD STREET c1938 B82018

Tickenhill Manor at Bewdley was given to the Mortimer family by William the Conqueror, coming back to the Crown at the time of Edward IV. Prince Arthur, the eldest son of Henry VII, married Catherine of Aragon here - by proxy, for she was an absent bride. Poor Arthur died young, leaving the throne and his wife to his younger brother, Henry VIII.

BEWDLEY, THE BRIDGE 1904 51976

Thomas Telford's stately bridge over the Severn was completed in 1801, a delightful mixture of stone and cast iron. An earlier bridge at Bewdley, described by the topographer Leland as a 'goodly fair bridge over Severn of great arches of stone', probably led to the development of the town.

BEWDLEY, THE RIVER c1938 B82009

In Saxon days the name of this place was Wribbenhall. The Normans, impressed with its setting, renamed it Beaulieu, 'the beautiful place'. In Tudor times the principal trade of Bewdley was the manufacture of caps. So important was this industry to the national economy that Elizabeth I banned the importation of caps from elsewhere, and decreed that all persons must wear caps on the Sabbath and holy days.

BEWDLEY, VIEW ON THE RIVER c1950 B82003

Stanley Baldwin, Prime Minister and on his retirement Earl Baldwin of Bewdley, represented the town as its Member of Parliament for many years. He loved Bewdley, and said 'I can turn back in memory and recollection to this peaceful spot by the side of the river, where I first drew breath, and in the memory of which I am able to draw strength'.

BEWDLEY, LOAD STREET c1955 B82032
St Anne's Church at the end of Load Street was originally a chantry chapel, said to have been built by fugitives so that they might claim sanctuary. The present church was built in 1746.

BEOLEY, THE POST OFFICE c1965 B845002
Beoley lies in rolling countryside just two miles north-east of Redditch. The estate belonged for many years to the Sheldon family. William Sheldon fought for Henry VII at Bosworth Field in 1485, but is better known for encouraging a renaissance in English tapestry, sending workmen abroad to learn the then lost art.

BRANSFORD
The Bank House and Motel c1965
Bransford's original bridge over the River Teme was built by a local cleric, Bishop Wulstan de Bransford, in 1338. Two of its three arches were destroyed during the Civil War, and a replacement now stands there. There are many lovely old buildings in the vicinity, such as Bank House.

BREDON
St Giles' Church c1955
The beautiful village of Bredon stands at the foot of Bredon Hill, and is deservedly on everyone's list of favourite English villages. The spire of the church is 160 feet high, and is almost as prominent a local landmark as the famous hill nearby.

BRANSFORD, THE BANK HOUSE AND MOTEL c1965 B421001

BREDON, ST GILES' CHURCH c1955 B423006

BREDON, THE VILLAGE c1955 B423040
Eanulf, grandfather of King Offa of Mercia, founded a monastery at Bredon, though nothing of it is to be seen. The present church owes its origins to the Normans and their influence, its medieval additions making it an architectural joy. Not far away is a 14th-century tithe barn, the second largest in England.

BROADWAS, THE VILLAGE c1955 B425003
Broadwas stands on a ridge, with wonderfully clear views across to the Malvern Hills. Some half a dozen miles west of Worcester, with the River Teme gently flowing not far away, Broadwas was a very quiet and seldom-visited place until the arrival of the motor car.

BROADWAS
The Post Office c1955
A car halts outside the village shop in Broadwas on an otherwise quiet day in the 1950s. Most visitors to Worcestershire still miss Broadwas, which is a pity, as it has elegant houses, a historic church and exceptional viewpoints.

BROADWAY
The Village and the New Church 1899
Broadway is a tempting village for tourists today, full of antique and craft shops. But its popularity does nothing to detract from the fact that this is an exceptionally beautiful Worcestershire village, each building in harmony with its neighbour and all constructed from the same warm local stone.

BROADWAS, THE POST OFFICE c1955 B425001

BROADWAY, THE VILLAGE AND THE NEW CHURCH 1899 44115

BROADWAY, THE VILLAGE 1899 44113

A number of the older houses here were originally inns, for Broadway lay on the London to Worcester coaching route. Here we can see the village in quieter days, before the constant stream of cars that flood into Broadway today. The heaviest traffic shown here is this horse-drawn covered wagon.

BROADWAY, CHINA SQUARE 1899 44117

Broadway has its place in history. Both Charles I and Oliver Cromwell stayed in the village during the Civil War. This tumble-down cottage had probably changed little since those stirring times.

BROMSGROVE, HIGH STREET 1931 84647
This old market town, famed for its manufacture of nails, is situated on the slopes of the Lickey Hills. Leland remarked that 'the towne of Bromsgrove is all in a manner of one street, very long, standing in a plaine ground'. Not quite so true today, though the High Street remains a lengthy walk of shops.

BROMSGROVE, ST JOHN'S STREET 1931 84649
There are some famous monuments in the church at Bromsgrove, many decorated with effigies and informative inscriptions. Amongst the earliest is the table tomb of Sir Humphrey Stafford of Grafton, who died in 1450 during Jack Cade's rebellion. Shakespeare, who probably visited Bromsgrove, depicted Stafford's end in 'Henry VI' Part II.

BROMSGROVE
High Street 1931 84648

Charles Stuart, fleeing after his defeat at the Battle of Worcester in 1651, reached Bromsgrove disguised as the servant of the remarkable Jane Lane. Charles found himself in the extraordinary position of having to denounce himself to the Parliamentarian blacksmith who was shoeing his horse. The smith congratulated the fugitive for being 'an honest man'.

BROMSGROVE, OLD TIMBERED HOUSES c1950 B233001

A favourite epitaph is that over the graves of Thomas Scaife and Joseph Rutherford, killed in a railway accident: 'My engine now is cold and still, No water does my boiler fill; My coke affords its flames no more; My days of usefulness are o'er'.

BUSHLEY, THE POST OFFICE c1960 B426012

Almost in Gloucestershire, Bushley lies but a couple of miles from Tewkesbury. That royal tigress Margaret of Anjou is said to have hidden at Paynes Place at Bushley after her defeat at the Battle of Tewkesbury in 1471.

BUSHLEY
The Old School House c1960
This lovely half-timbered house is typical of many houses in this quiet neighbourhood, not far from the banks of the River Severn. Much of the land hereabouts belonged to the Dowdeswell family for hundreds of years. Bushley Church is full of their monuments, including that of General William Dowdeswell who fought against Napoleon.

◆

CASTLE MORTON
The Church c1960
Once known as Morton Foliot, the parish of Castle Morton runs a long way up to the Malvern Hills. St Gregory's Church dates from the 12th to the 14th centuries. A low mound is all that remains of the castle that gave the village its name.

BUSHLEY, THE OLD SCHOOL HOUSE c1960 B426015

CASTLE MORTON, THE CHURCH c1960 C499004

CASTLE MORTON, THE POST OFFICE c1960 C499001
Despite some modern buildings, Castle Morton is a village of great charm. Its ancient Common is still a good place for a wander as you admire the Malverns a few miles away.

CASTLE MORTON, YE OLD ROBIN HOOD c1960 C499007
Castle Morton has no real known link with England's most famous outlaw, though Robin Hood features as a place name all over the Midlands and the North. This sometime inn pays him an honour not granted to many local worthies.

CHADDESLEY CORBETT, HARVINGTON HALL c1965 C328006

Harvington Hall is a mile from the village of Chaddesley Corbett; it is a fine moated manor house mostly dating back to the 16th century. The Pakington family, who held the house in the troubled times of Catholic persecution, often hid priests in the many secret chambers within the old house.

CHADDESLEY CORBETT, THE YHA AND THE SWAN HOTEL c1965 C328012

This one-street town is one of the most delightful in England; it is a special place to visit and an even better one to stay in, to use as a base for the exploration of Worcestershire. The Youth Hostel, seen here on the left, is sadly no longer a part of the YHA network.

CHADDESLEY CORBETT, THE TALBOT INN c1965 C328017

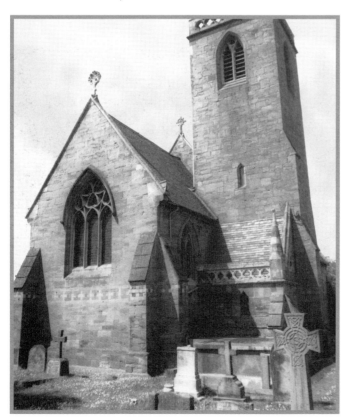

CHURCHILL, THE CHURCH c1960 C334004

CHADDESLEY CORBETT
The Talbot Inn c1965
Some consider the Talbot Inn to be the best, in architectural terms, in the whole of the county, and even the finest in England. This beautiful half-timbered inn is even more of a joy given its setting amongst so many other unspoiled buildings.

◆

CHURCHILL
The Church c1960
This church was badly restored by the Victorians in 1863, though many of its historic portions were spared. In the churchyard is the mass grave of nuns of the Order of Poor Clares, who fled here from Dunkirk during the French Revolution.

CLIFTON UPON TEME
Ham Bridge c1965

Clifton upon Teme's name is rather misleading, for the village itself stands a considerable distance from that river. Many visitors come to the church to see the 13th-century tomb of Ralph Wysham, his feet resting on a dog - which is supposedly how his body was found, feet resting on a favourite hound, when the Lord of the Manor failed to return from a country walk.

◆

CROPTHORNE
The Village 1901

At the south-eastern corner of Worcestershire stands Cropthorne, a pretty village just off the Evesham to Pershore road. Its old cottages with their colourful gardens, its ancient church, and lovely scenery with Bredon Hill just in the background, make a visit a memorable experience.

CLIFTON UPON TEME, HAM BRIDGE c1965 C331003

CROPTHORNE, THE VILLAGE 1901 47321

CROPTHORNE, THE MILL 1910 62353
Situated on the Avon, Cropthorne Mill has often attracted the attentions of artists and photographers. The woman and child are crossing the river by way of a chain ferry, pulling themselves across on a fixed cable - almost the oldest form of regular river crossing in England.

DROITWICH, THE OLD COCK INN c1910 D54003

Droitwich developed as a spa in the early 19th century thanks to John Corbett, a local businessman, who opened the St Andrews Brine Baths in the town for visitors, and built a magnificent French-style chateau just outside for himself. Not everyone drank the waters. The sign here says 'The Old Cock Inn, by Walter Harrison, licensed in the tenth year of the reign of Queen Anne. Retailer of foreign Wines and Spirits'.

DROITWICH, 1931 84632

Towards the end of the 20th century, the population of Droitwich increased when the town took some of the overspill from Birmingham. Fortunately, much of the town centre has survived the worst excesses of the developer.

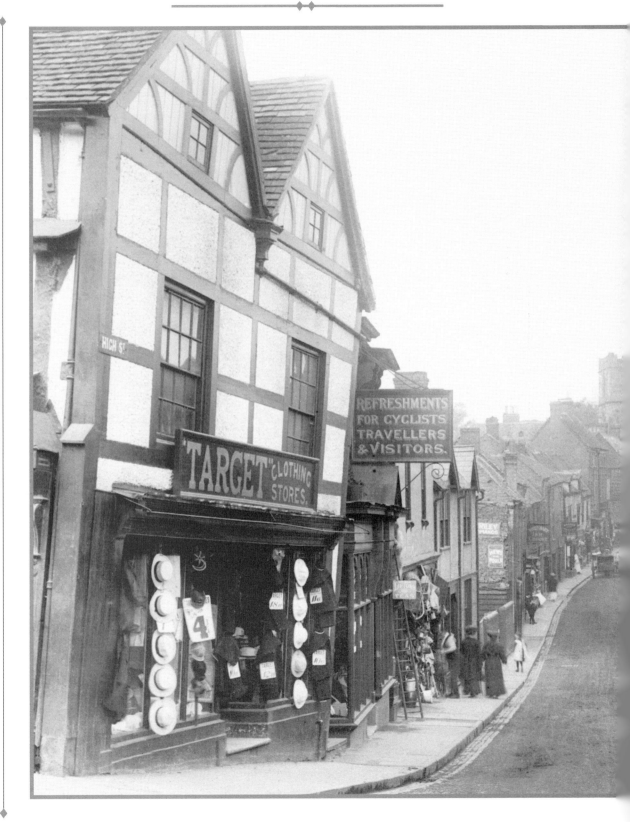

DROITWICH
High Street 1904 51938
The spring water rising from beneath Droitwich is said
to be 10 times saltier than the ocean and even saltier
than the Dead Sea. The Romans knew of these
springs, and called their settlement Salinae. The Droit
(land held by right) was added to the Saxon Wic to
give the town its present name.

ELMLEY CASTLE, THE VILLAGE c1955 E108019

Elmley Castle is one of those delightful villages lying around the foot of Bredon Hill. Little now remains of the castle itself, once the stronghold of the Beauchamp family. The inn sign features a portrait of Queen Elizabeth on one side and an illustration of her arriving to stay at the inn on the other. It appears she really did sleep here.

ELMLEY CASTLE, THE VILLAGE c1960 E108001

Leland the traveller recorded that only one tower and a little stonework from the castle remained at the time of his visit. Even as he watched, bits of castle were taken away: 'I saw carts carienge stone thens to amend Pershore Bridge', he commented.

EVESHAM

The Bell Tower from the Avon 1892 31088
At the centre of a broad vale, rich in
market gardens and fruit orchards, and
to which it gives its name, lies Evesham.
Abbot Lichfield's Bell Tower, built in
1539, dominates the water meadows of
the River Avon. Notice the Romany
caravans at rest on the far bank.

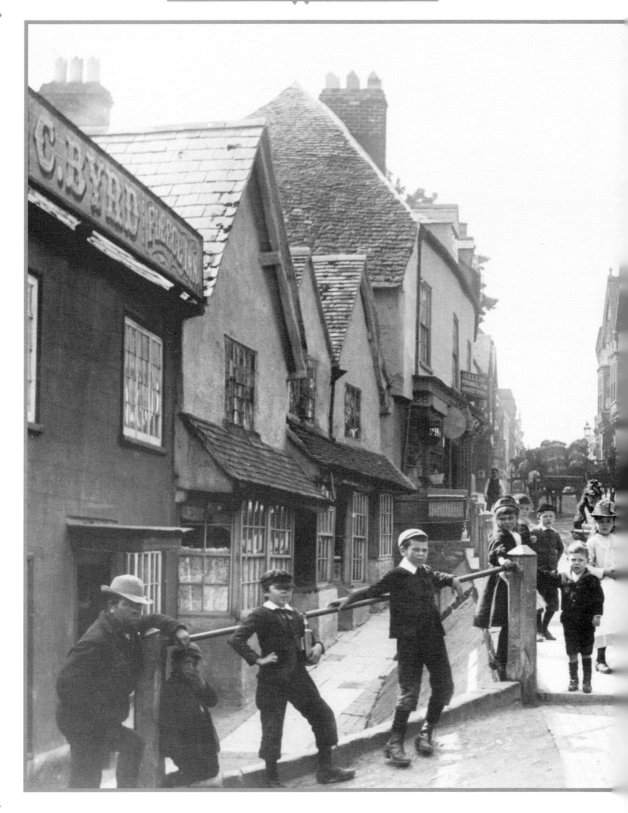

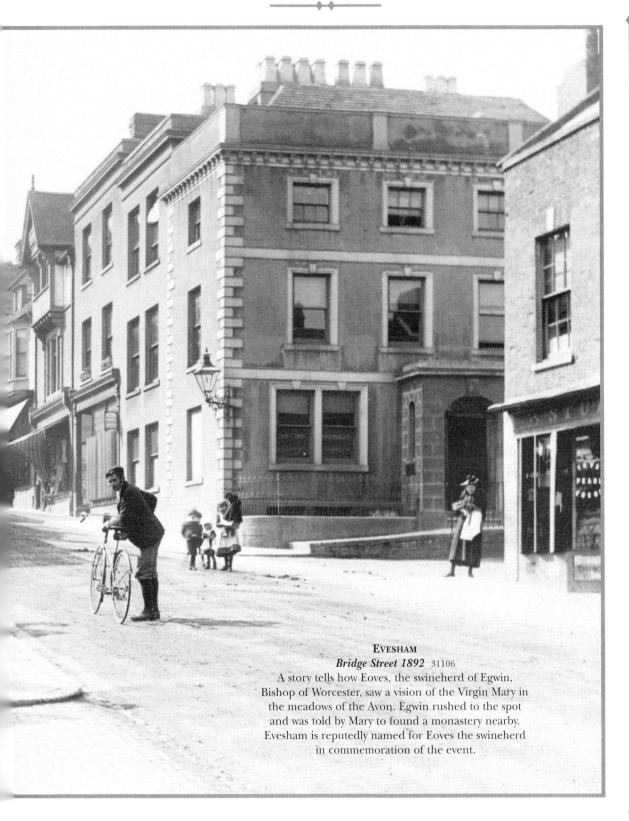

EVESHAM
Bridge Street 1892 31106
A story tells how Eoves, the swineherd of Egwin,
Bishop of Worcester, saw a vision of the Virgin Mary in
the meadows of the Avon. Egwin rushed to the spot
and was told by Mary to found a monastery nearby.
Evesham is reputedly named for Eoves the swineherd
in commemoration of the event.

EVESHAM, THE THREE SPIRES 1892 31089
Three children play against the superb backdrop of some of the best ecclesiastical architecture in Worcestershire.
Evesham's two churches share the same churchyard. Abbot Lichfield, who built the Bell Tower, did not enjoy his
creation for very long. Evesham Abbey was dissolved by Henry VIII in 1539 - the same year that the tower
was completed.

EVESHAM
Hampton Ferry 1895

The countryside around Evesham has not always been so peaceful. On 4 August 1265, during a thunderstorm as fierce as the battle on the ground beneath, Henry III defeated the rebel barons commanded by Simon de Montfort. It is said that over 4000 men, including de Montfort and his son, perished in the slaughter.

EVESHAM
Chadbury Mill 1899

Evesham is a good place to begin an exploration of the Vale around, the River Avon and the not too distant Cotswolds. As befits an important agricultural area, a number of mills prospered on the banks of the River Avon - an inspiration to every passing artist and photographer.

EVESHAM, HAMPTON FERRY 1895   36969

EVESHAM, CHADBURY MILL 1899   44120

EVESHAM
High Street 1910 62339
It is a peaceful day in Evesham at the end of Edward VII's reign, with some good examples of shop signs, such as Deakin's fruit and marmalade, 'the best that skill and science can provide', and G.F.B.'s premier tea, 'specially blended to suit Evesham water'.

EVESHAM, CHURCH HOUSES 1910 62349
The street patterns of Evesham have probably changed little since the days of the battle, when many of the rebels fleeing from that desperate fight were slaughtered amongst its houses. It is easy to see here how the Bell Tower dominates the neighbourhood - it was originally designed partly as a landmark to attract and guide the faithful across the Vale of Evesham.

FECKENHAM, THE VILLAGE c1960 F655221

Feckenham once stood at the heart of Feckenham Forest, an ancient hunting ground of kings, which once covered some 200 square miles and included over 60 settlements. The last of the timber disappeared in the 17th century, into the hungry furnaces of nearby Droitwich. Tobacco cultivation replaced the trees, thriving until its production was made illegal.

FECKENHAM, THE PARISH CHURCH c1960 F655222

A local preacher, John of Feckenham, became a monk at nearby Evesham. After the Dissolution, he spent some years in the Tower of London before becoming Abbot of Westminster under Queen Mary. Even her Protestant sister Elizabeth I loved the old monk; on her succession, she pleaded with John to give up Catholicism and become her Dean. He refused, but was placed on parole - a gentle punishment for that time - and spent the rest of his life drifting around England in self-imposed imprisonment until his death at Wisbech.

FECKENHAM, THE WATERFALL c1960 F655223

FECKENHAM
The Waterfall c1960
This little scene of timber and water gives a feeling of how tranquil the Forest of Feckenham must have been when it covered the hills and vales round about. The rivers and ponds of Worcestershire are still much appreciated by the angler seeking the peace and quiet of the countryside.

◆

FLADBURY
The Lock and Ferry 1902
Fladbury was the site of a Saxon monastery, though nothing of it remains; the existing parish church is mostly 14th century. Across the Avon from Cropthorne, Fladbury is situated in rolling agricultural land of pasture and orchard.

FLADBURY, THE LOCK AND FERRY 1902 47319

FLADBURY, THE WEIR c1960 F1415286

Yet another of Worcestershire's imposing old mills stands on the banks of the River Avon near to Fladbury. A walk along the county's rivers will reveal many other mills - a delight to the eye and a temptation for the camera.

GREAT COMBERTON, THE VILLAGE c1960 G331014

The old parish of Great Comberton runs from the river Avon to the summit of Bredon Hill. In its church is a memorial to Edmund Smith and his family, all drowned in the wreck of the 'Royal Charter' in 1859, as they journeyed home from Australia.

GREAT MALVERN, THE MALVERN RANGE FROM THE CAMP HILL C1874 7071B

Great Malvern village is set against the stunning backdrop of the Malvern Hills, that great range of summits that rises above the surrounding plains of Worcestershire; they form one of the finest ridge walks in England, with extensive views all the way across the Midlands, the Border Marches and Wales.

GREAT MALVERN, THE PRIORY CHURCH 1893 32387

At the time of Domesday Book, this part of Worcestershire was described as a 'wilderness', with 'numerous and vast thickets'. Great Malvern grew up around a Benedictine Priory said to have been founded by St Wrest, who found sanctuary here from marauding Danes.

GREAT MALVERN
The Abbey Gate 1893

Only the Priory Church and Gatehouse remain; the rest of the buildings were taken down in the aftermath of Henry VIII's Dissolution. Thomas Cromwell, the architect of this destruction, was charitable towards the occupants, giving pensions to the Prior and eleven monks.

◆

GREAT MALVERN
The College 1893

Malvern College for Boys was founded in 1865 and is one of England's leading public schools. Many of the early pupils were the children of parents scattered across the British Empire. Notice the horse-drawn lawnmower in the foreground.

GREAT MALVERN, THE ABBEY GATE 1893 32394

GREAT MALVERN, THE COLLEGE 1893 32406

GREAT MALVERN, WYNDSPOINT 1893 32407s

'The Vision Concerning Piers the Plowman' by William Langland was inspired by the Malvern Hills, and remains one of the most important early works of English literature, with its vivid portrayal of 14th-century life. On a fine and clear day it is not hard to recapture the 'Vision' from the summit of the hills. Wyndspoint was once the home of the singer and musical patron Jenny Lind, the 'Swedish Nightingale'.

GREAT MALVERN, FROM THE CHURCH TOWER 1899 43988

William Langland was probably a monk at Malvern Priory, or some minor religious house thereabouts. He was born in 1332 at Ledbury, the illegitimate son of a Worcestershire worthy called Stacy de Rokayle. Langland's immortal poem gives us an excellent feel of just what people were like seven hundred years ago, rivalling Chaucer's 'Canterbury Tales'.

GREAT MALVERN, FROM THE CHURCH TOWER 1899 43989
It is little wonder that this restful landscape has inspired great art. Sir Edward Elgar is buried at Little Malvern. Elgar was a true son of Worcestershire, and much of his music was inspired by his regular walks around the Malvern Hills.

MALVERN WELLS, HOLYWELL 1904 51153
The medicinal values of the waters around Malvern have been known to local people for centuries, and Doctor John Wall published a treatise on their efficacy in 1756. Holy Well was renowned for its treatment of people with eye problems; bottling of the water began as early as 1622. Dickens, Carlyle, Gladstone and Florence Nightingale all came to Malvern to 'take the cure'.

MALVERN WELLS

General View 1907 59029

As with so many places in England, the coming of the railway in the 1840s made Malvern's fortune, bringing visitors from far and wide. Despite this early appearance by a motor car, it was to be several decades before the advent of popular motoring made Malvern the tourist destination we know today.

GREAT MALVERN, THE BRITISH CAMP HOTEL 1907 59023

The medicinal regime was quite severe during its Victorian heyday. In the 1840s patients at the health centre of Dr Wilson and Dr Gully were subjected to strict dieting, long walks over the hills and the indignity of being wrapped up in cold wet sheets for hours at a time.

GREAT WITLEY, WITLEY COURT 1911 64053

Witley Court was one of England's grandest stately homes. The land around once belonged to the Cookesey family, but was bought in the 1600s by Thomas Foley, who had made his fortune in the iron trade. His grandson, Lord Foley, built this mansion in the Italian style in 1725. This lovely old building burnt to the ground in 1937.

GREAT WITLEY, WITLEY COURT, CHURCH INTERIOR c1965 G143002
It is fortunate that the church at Witley, built by Lady Foley in 1735, and decorated under the guidance of the artistic Earl of Dudley, survived the fire. Its rich and embellished interior makes Witley Church a 'must' for any visitor to Worcestershire.

GREAT WITLEY, HUNDRED HOUSE c1965 G143008
This red-brick Georgian coaching inn stands at the centre of Great Witley. The village is situated in a pleasant spot just below the Abberley Hills, an outcrop of the Malverns. There is a great deal of attractive countryside to explore nearby.

HARTLEBURY, GYPSY CARAVANS, WORCESTER COUNTY MUSEUM c1965 H376008

Both this gypsy vardo, or travelling wagon, and Mr Robbins' old farm cart would have been familiar to earlier generations as they travelled the lanes of Worcestershire. Both wagons were originally part of the collection of J F Parker of Bewdley, transferred after his death to the Worcester County Museum.

HARTLEBURY, A FARM WAGON, WORCESTER COUNTY MUSEUM c1965 H376012

HOLT FLEET, THE HOTEL 1906 54292
The tea gardens and inns which line the banks of the Severn are a favourite place to pause for locals and visitor alike. Holt Bridge, nearby, is the last bridge across the river before Worcester, a good place to begin a river trip.

HALLOW, THE GREEN 1911 64054
Hallow is sited just a couple of miles north-west of Worcester. Queen Elizabeth I certainly visited Hallow on her Royal Progress around the county. The horses belonging to her retinue grazed the local pastures during this visit.

HALLOW
The Green c1955 H152009
Inside the church is a monument to Sir Charles Bell, whose only connection with Hallow is that he died there on a visit in 1842. Bell, who achieved fame for treating the wounded after the Battle of Waterloo, is best known for discovering how the body's nervous system works.

HALLOW
The Crown Inn c1955
The Crown Inn at Hallow was a popular venue for the motoring public visiting from nearby Worcester. It has often been a place to halt for racegoers after a day at the nearby Worcester racecourse.

HALLOW, THE CROWN INN c1955 H152008

HANBURY, MAIN ROAD c1965 H501012

HANBURY
Main Road c1965

A monastery stood at Hanbury in Anglo-Saxon times, when the land came into the possession of the Church at Worcester. There is now no trace of the original religious buildings. Hanbury's present church has many imposing monuments to the Vernon family, who lived nearby at Hanbury Hall.

◆

HANBURY
A Thatched Cottage c1965

Worcestershire is fortunate to have many thousands of delightful buildings, a number of which are of considerable antiquity. This thatched cottage at Hanbury probably started its existence as a humble home for a farm labourer, and was added to as the years went by.

HANBURY, A THATCHED COTTAGE c1965 H501004

HOLT FLEET, THE BRIDGE 1906 54294
Visitors who halt for a while here may walk a little way to the village of Holt. There is the much-restored Holt Castle and a church dating back to the 14th century to see.

KEMPSEY, THE CHURCH 1892 29894
St Mary's Church at Kempsey lies close to the banks of the River Severn, a few miles south of Worcester. Much of this interesting cross church dates back to the 13th century. A monastery which stood here in the 9th century was given to the Church of Worcester. Worcester's Bishop had a summer palace close to Kempsey Church.

KEMPSEY, THE VILLAGE 1892 29897
Kempsey's church, seen here through the trees, has a puzzling 18th-century monument inside, which reads 'Underneath the corruptible parts of a vicar, one husband, two helpmeets, both wives and both Anns, a triplicity of persons in two twains but one flesh, are interred'.

KEMPSEY, THE RIVER AND THE CHURCH 1910 62361
A parish clerk of Kempsey Church once caught a choir-boy eating chestnuts inside the building. The clerk confiscated the last chestnut, carelessly throwing it away in the vicinity of the tomb of Sir Edmund Wylde, where it fell into a dust-filled cranny. It took root, and for some sixty years a chestnut tree grew within the church.

KEMPSEY, THE VILLAGE 1910 62358
Kempsey's inhabitants must have been fond of trees. Tombs within the church commemorate two villagers, John White and John Capel, who planted over 60,000 trees during their respective careers.

KIDDERMINSTER, THE TOWN HALL AND THE SWAN HOTEL 1931 84610

Kidderminster owes its fame to the manufacture of carpets, but had prospered from the weaving trade long before that. Flemish weavers began to arrive in the town in the 13th century, at about the time that Kidderminster became a borough. Within a century, the town was one of the leading cloth-producing centres in Europe. The statue seen here is of Sir Rowland Hill, creator of the penny post.

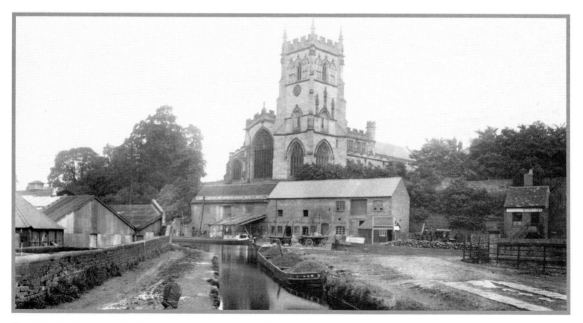

KIDDERMINSTER, THE CHURCH AND THE CANAL 1931 84619

The carpet industry began here in the 1700s, when a Mr Pearsall built the first factory for their production. Pearsall took advantage of the new handlooms developed by John Broom, a local entrepreneur. In later years, both the River Stour and the associated canal system were used to transport carpets on the first stage of their journeys to the marketplaces of the world.

KIDDERMINSTER, HIGH STREET c1955 K16008

Rowland Hill was born in Kidderminster in 1795. As a young impoverished man he dreaded the postman's knock on his door, for letters had to be paid for on delivery. This embarrassment caused him to lower postage rates by introducing pre-paid postage stamps for letters.

KIDDERMINSTER, TOWN CENTRE c1960 K16025

By the 1960s, the increase in motor cars started to cause problems in the narrow streets of Kidderminster, though the dreaded yellow lines had yet to appear. Notice the very convenient bad-weather shelter for the policeman on point duty.

KIDDERMINSTER
St Mary's Church c1960

Kidderminster's late-medieval church is built in the attractive local red sandstone. There are some interesting monuments within, including a triple brass for Sir John Phelip, his wife Matilda and her first husband, Sir Walter Cokesey. Sir John fought at Harfleur in 1415 during Henry V's invasion of France. His second wife was the granddaughter of the poet Geoffrey Chaucer.

◆

KIDDERMINSTER
Peckett Rock, Habberley Valley c1960

Kidderminster is an excellent centre for visiting northern Worcestershire, with some fascinating villages and beautiful scenery nearby. Habberley Valley, on the outskirts of town, is popular with locals and tourists alike.

KIDDERMINSTER, ST MARY'S CHURCH c1960   K16046

KIDDERMINSTER, PECKETT ROCK, HABBERLEY VALLEY c1960   K16054

KING'S NORTON, THE OLD SARACENS HEAD 1949 K83007

King's Norton, 'a praty uplandyshe towne', according to the topographer Leland, lies a few miles south of Birmingham, to which city - rather than Worcestershire - it now belongs. Leland recorded that 'there is a faire churche and a goodly piramis of stone over the bell frame'.

KING'S NORTON, THE VILLAGE GREEN C1955 K83008

In 1086 King's Norton belonged to the Royal Manor of Bromsgrove, remaining in the possession of the Crown until the beginning of the 19th century. Despite becoming a suburb of Birmingham in the 20th century, it retains quite a village atmosphere.

LITTLE COMBERTON, THE VILLAGE c1955 L216003
Little Comberton lies on the northern side of Bredon Hill, not far from its sister village of Great Comberton. This pastoral area has long been settled by humankind, for Roman coins and pottery have been found nearby. Its cottages are some of the prettiest in Worcestershire.

LITTLE COMBERTON, THE VILLAGE c1955 L216005

In recent years Little Comberton has become a larger settlement than Great Comberton, though it is debatable which has the loveliest buildings. Parts of Little Comberton's church date back to at least the 12th century, though there was considerable rebuilding in 1887.

LITTLE COMBERTON, THE OLDE THATCHED COTTAGE c1955 L216007

Even olde thatched cottages were displaying aerials by the 1950s. This half-timbered building with its thatched porch and gateway is one of the oldest in Little Comberton.

LONGDON
The Moat House c1960

The village of Longdon lies on the western edge of some high ground, separating Longdon Marsh from the River Severn. The low-lying ground around here was once part of the Severn's tidal estuary, and some saltwater plants can still be found. The moat of this old property was filled in some years ago.

◆

LONGDON
Moat Bank c1960

Longdon's church, seen here behind the trees, has a tower and spire dating from the 14th century. Much of the rest of the building was replaced in the 18th and 19th centuries. There has been a great deal of modern building in the village, though many of Longdon's half-timbered houses have survived.

LONGDON, THE MOAT HOUSE C1960 L217002

LONGDON, MOAT BANK C1960 L217004

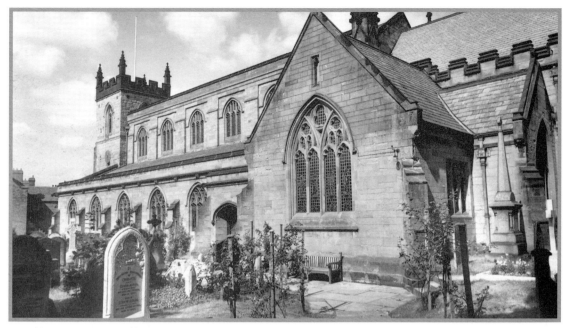

MOSELEY, ST MARY'S CHURCH c1955 M154003
Rather like King's Norton, Moseley appears in Domesday Book as a berewick of the Royal Manor of Bromsgrove.
Part of the church dates back to around 1400, though there have been a great many later additions. Moseley,
a mere two miles south of Birmingham, has now become a suburb of that great city.

NORTH LITTLETON, THE VILLAGE c1960 N220013
The Littletons - North, Middle and South - form almost one long village in the countryside close to Evesham. They
are set in a land of rolling countryside, orchards and charming buildings - such as the ones seen here.

OMBERSLEY, THE VILLAGE 1899 44016

An evangelical mission wagon lies idle in the quiet village street. This large parish runs along the eastern bank of the Severn for several miles. There is some quite stunning 16th- and 17th-century architecture.

OMBERSLEY, THE VILLAGE 1910 62631

Evesham Abbey held the Manor of Ombersley for several centuries until the Dissolution, its abbots often residing there. In the early 17th century it came into the possession of the Sandys family. Three veterans of Waterloo are commemorated in the church, including Lord Sandys, aide-de-camp to the Duke of Wellington.

PERSHORE, FROM AVONBANK 1931 84669

PERSHORE
From Avonbank 1931
Pershore is an old market town of considerable charm on the right bank of the River Avon. Its medieval bridge was badly damaged during the Civil War, but was soon restored to its former glory.

PERSHORE
Lower Newlands 1931
A religious house was founded in Pershore in about 689. The Normans transformed the Benedictine abbey into one of England's greatest Christian establishments, the abbey building being larger than Worcester Cathedral. It was destroyed at the Reformation.

PERSHORE, LOWER NEWLANDS 1931 84675

PERSHORE, BRIDGE STREET 1931 84678
Much of the architecture of this country town is Georgian, though there are a few older buildings. The Angel Hotel, seen here, is an ancient posting inn, carefully restored a decade before this photograph was taken. Since the dissolution of its abbey, Pershore has prospered from fruit-growing.

PERSHORE, BROAD STREET C1955 P45009
Pershore's Fair began in the reign of Henry III to provide funds for the restoration of the presbytery. It was held in the churchyard until the mid 1800s. Merchants would come from right across the Vale of Evesham and the Cotswolds to sell their wares. Local villagers still make their way to Pershore for their shopping at least once a week.

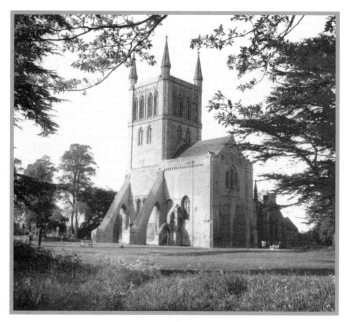

PERSHORE, THE ABBEY C1960 P45048

PERSHORE
The Abbey c1960
This truncated church is all that remains of the great abbey that once stood on this site. An old fishpond of the monks may still be seen, but gardens and greenery now cover the foundations of the nave and cloisters.

POWICK
The Village 1906
Powick stands where the waters of the Severn and the Teme mingle. Everyone who loves fine porcelain should visit Powick, for it was the birthplace in 1708 of Dr John Wall, who opened the first factory for the creation of Worcester Porcelain.

POWICK, THE VILLAGE 1906 54289

POWICK, THE OLD BRIDGE 1906 54290

Powick's older bridge was the scene of a Civil War battle in 1651 when Royalist troops under Montgomery held it for two hours against superior Parliamentary forces. Montgomery and his men fought courageously, but were eventually overwhelmed.

POWICK, POWYKE ASYLUM 1910 62366

This extensive and grim asylum is a reminder of how earlier generations treated the mentally-ill by locking them away, often far from their homes and families. It remains a functional, if forbidding, example of Victorian architecture.

POWICK, THE VILLAGE c1950 P108501

Much of the quietness of old Powick was lost for ever in the 20th century when a new road from Malvern to Worcester was cut through the parish. But the countryside around remains largely unspoiled and full of reminders of the battles and skirmishes of the English Civil War.

REDDITCH, ALCESTER ROAD 1949 R84013

Redditch appears in an ancient document describing the Perambulation of Feckenham Forest in 1300 as Le Red Dych. The town became unimportant after the Dissolution, with the evacuation of nearby Bordesley Abbey, only regaining its former status in the first part of the 19th century.

REDDITCH, EVESHAM STREET c1955 R84007

Just a few miles south of the industrial Midlands, Redditch became famous for the manufacture of needles, fishhooks and bicycles. Many new industries have come to Redditch since this photograph was taken.

RIBBESFORD, THE HOUSE c1965 R269001

This charming woodland parish without a village covers parts of the banks of the River Severn. The great house belonged originally to the de Ribbesfords. In the 17th century, Charles I gave it to the three Herbert brothers, one of whom was George Herbert the poet.

RIBBESFORD, THE LIDO CAFÉ c1965 R269006
During the days of early popular motoring, the fine scenery in the valley of the Severn attracted many day-trippers from the urban areas of the Midlands. The Lido Café was a much frequented leisure stop along the way.

SHRAWLEY, THE MONASTERY c1960 S385001
Shrawley is a very ancient settlement, its woodlands sloping down to the River Severn. Not far away was once a Norman castle, strategically placed to guard the river valley; it was occupied until the downfall of Warwick the Kingmaker, who owned it in the 15th century. The ruins can still be visited.

SOUTH LITTLETON, HIGH STREET c1960 S386001

Not far from Evesham, South Littleton is a lovely old village of pretty cottages, a manor house built in 1721, though attached to an even more ancient building, and a church that originally dated back to Norman times.

SOUTH LITTLETON, THE OLD TITHE BARN c1960 S386009

South Littleton's splendid tithe barn is a relic of those times when a tenth (tithe) of the harvest had to be given to the Church, which held considerable power over the medieval community.

STANFORD BRIDGE, THE HOTEL, THE POST OFFICE AND STORE c1955 S387012
Stanford-on-Teme, eight miles from Stourport and not far from the border of Herefordshire, stands on a very old crossing point on the Teme. A mile away is Southstone Rock, a great mass of travertine lining a steep gorge; the site of a medieval hermitage and chapel

STANFORD BRIDGE, THE BRIDGE AND MILL FARM c1955 S387009
A bronze tablet removed from an earlier bridge reads: 'Pray for Humfrey Pakynton Esquyer borne in Stanford which payde for ye workemanshepe and makyng of this brygg the whiche was rered & made the first day of May and in the first yere of ye rayne of Kyng Edward ye VIth'.

STANFORD BRIDGE, THE BRIDGE AND THE MILL c1960 S387005

The mill seen here on the right is of considerable antiquity, even in this village of old buildings. A little further up the road is Stanford Court, once the home of the Winnington family. In 1769 the original village church was submerged so that the powerful landowner could construct a lake in front of his home. The new church has many memorials transported from the older building.

STANFORD BRIDGE, THE VILLAGE c1960 S387001

Stanford's rectory was the birthplace in 1775 of the author and moralist Mrs Sherwood, whose novel 'The Fairchild Family' was a popular improving text with the more rigidly censorious readers of Regency and early Victorian society. After a long period in India, Mrs Sherwood returned to Worcestershire and opened a school for young ladies.

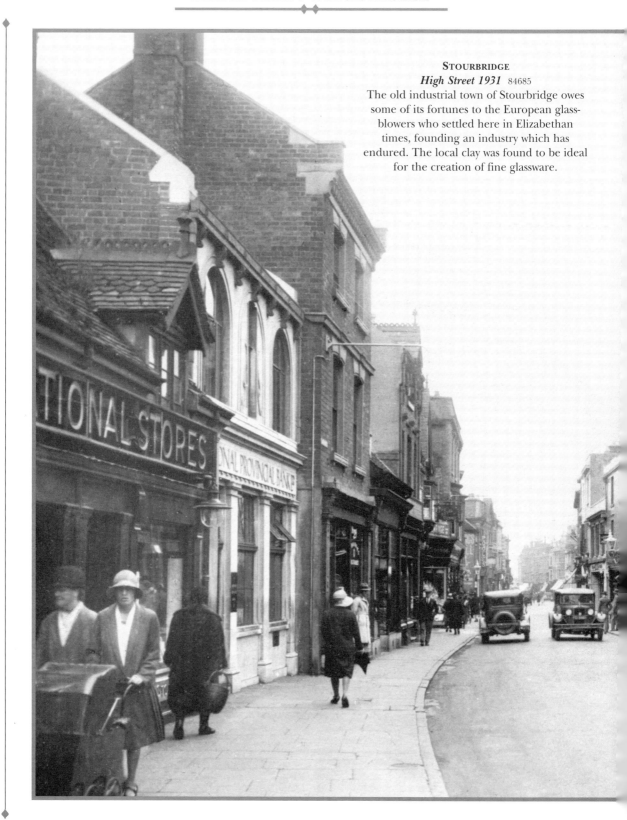

STOURBRIDGE
High Street 1931 84685
The old industrial town of Stourbridge owes
some of its fortunes to the European glass-
blowers who settled here in Elizabethan
times, founding an industry which has
endured. The local clay was found to be ideal
for the creation of fine glassware.

STOURBRIDGE, HIGH STREET 1931 84688
Up to the reign of Henry VI Stourbridge was called Bedcote, not taking its present name until 1454. It is unclear how long this settlement has existed, though some claim it was a village at the time when King Offa ruled Mercia.

STOKE PRIOR, THE CANAL c1965 S768008
Salt springs were discovered at Stoke Prior in 1828, and were developed by the Georgian entrepreneur John Corbett. The canal was used to facilitate the transportation of salt all around Britain.

STOURPORT-ON-SEVERN, THE BRIDGE 1904 51974

Stourport stands where the river Stour meets the Severn; it grew in importance after James Brindley built a canal junction there in the 1760s. The meeting of all these waterways proved important in the industrial development of the region. The rivers and canal are used for pleasure boating these days.

STOURPORT-ON-SEVERN, VIEW FROM THE BRIDGE 1931 84627

Stourport grew around the former village of Little Mitton by a stroke of fortune. Brindley originally wanted to bring his canal to the Severn at Bewdley, but the locals there objected to the very idea of such a 'stinking ditch'. Their obstinacy led to the creation of Stourport. The House of Laughter, seen here on the right, offers 'laughter with a scream, one penny only'.

STOURPORT-ON-SEVERN, VIEW FROM THE BRIDGE 1931 84626

These two river views shows how little the river scenery around Stourport changed over 25 years in the last century. Stourport's close proximity to the industrial cities of the Midlands made the town and the rivers a favourite day out around this period.

STOURPORT-ON-SEVERN, VIEW FROM THE BRIDGE c1955 S214022

STOURPORT-ON-SEVERN, THE ROCK CAVES 1931 84630
The soft rock cliffs above the Severn led to the creation of many caves. Some of these were enlarged and used as dwellings until quite recent times. They are now the haunt of visitors, strolling out from the nearby towns.

STOURPORT-ON-SEVERN, BRIDGE STREET c1955 S214027
Before James Brindley's arrival much of the site of modern Stourport was just sandy common land, with a solitary inn and a ferry crossing point. Within a few years a great industrial town had grown up around the confluence of the Stour and the Severn.

TENBURY WELLS, THE CHURCH 1892 30851A

The River Teme rises in Wales and flows through Shropshire before entering Worcestershire at Tenbury. This outstanding Norman church was undermined by the river in the floods of 1770, threatening the many superb memorials to Tenbury worthies of earlier days.

TENBURY WELLS, THE ROYAL OAK INN 1892 30849

Tenbury received its first charter for a market and fair in 1249, but remained a fairly humble country town until 1839 when a medicinal spring was discovered, leading to the creation of a pump room and spa, which was soon patronised by fashionable society.

TENBURY WELLS, MARKET STREET 1898 41720

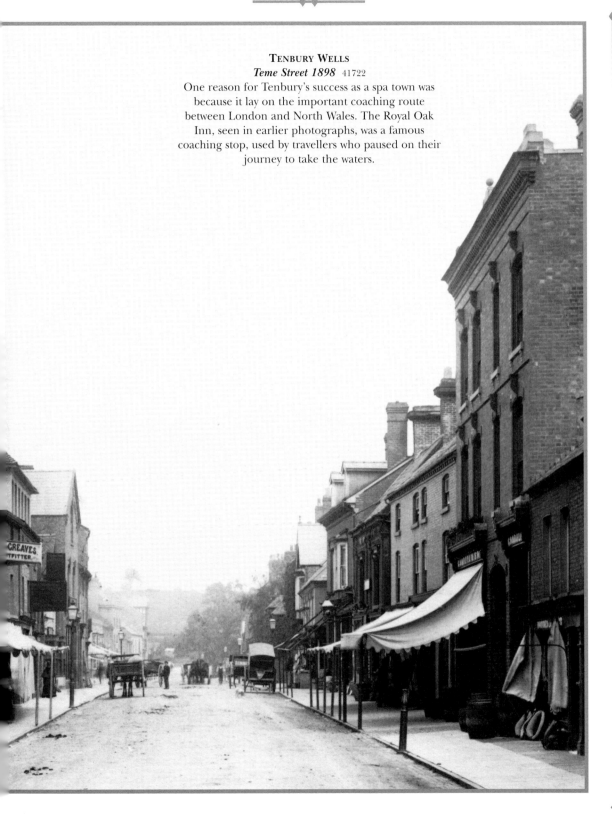

TENBURY WELLS
Teme Street 1898 41722
One reason for Tenbury's success as a spa town was because it lay on the important coaching route between London and North Wales. The Royal Oak Inn, seen in earlier photographs, was a famous coaching stop, used by travellers who paused on their journey to take the waters.

TENBURY WELLS, TEME STREET 1898 41723
Tenbury lies at the centre of a countryside rich in small farms, orchards and market gardens. Tenbury Wells is known even now as the 'town in the orchard'. Tenbury's fortunes as a spa town were mixed, and the pump room finally closed in 1939. It remains, however, an excellent centre for exploring Worcestershire and Shropshire.

TENBURY WELLS, OLD HOUSES 1898 41725
Tenbury boasts some excellent architecture, and a walk around its streets is a must for any visitor to Worcestershire. The sign above the third doorway from the left says 'Fire Engine Keys Kept Here'.

TENBURY WELLS, TEME BRIDGE 1898 41727A

Cattle seek the cool waters of the River Teme. After its journey through Wales, the river meanders through Shropshire and Worcestershire before joining the River Severn at Worcester. The scenery throughout this long journey is a delight.

TENBURY WELLS, COURT OF HILL 1898 41738

There are many fine buildings in this north-western corner of Worcestershire, such as Court of Hill, near Tenbury Wells. Notice the Victorian window shadings designed to keep the sun away from south-facing rooms.

TENBURY WELLS, THE ROYAL OAK HOTEL c1955 T22054

By the middle of the 20th century, this old coaching inn had geared itself up to cater for motorised tourists, winning the approval of the RAC (Royal Automobile Club) for its services. Notice how 'antiquated' windows have been added, compared to those in earlier photographs.

TENBURY WELLS, THE SQUARE c1955 T22056

The sign on the market building reads 'Cattell and Young: Auctioneers and Valuers; Weekly Produce Auction Every Tuesday'.

TIBBERTON, THE APPROACH TO THE CHURCH c1960 T161501
Tibberton is situated to the north-east of Worcester on the line of the Birmingham to Worcester Canal. This Victorian church, though interesting in its own way, is a poor substitute for the 13th-century structure demolished to make way for its construction.

TIBBERTON, A VIEW FROM THE BRIDGE c1960 T161502
Even by the 1960s the heyday of canals such as the Birmingham to Worcester was long past. But with their purely commercial use at an end, the canals of the Midlands have become popular for recreation and havens for wildlife.

TIBBERTON, MAIN ROAD c1960 T161503
During the latter half of the 20th century, villages such as Tibberton became favoured places to live for people working in neighbouring cities. New buildings appeared for commuting residents.

UPTON-ON-SEVERN, THE BRIDGE 1904 51968
Upton-on-Severn is a pleasant country town on the right bank of the Severn, some ten miles south of Worcester. It was once a flourishing port and suffered in the skirmishings before the Battle of Worcester, when the church and old bridge were badly damaged.

UPTON-ON-SEVERN, THE BRIDGE 1904 51967

The novelist Henry Fielding knew Upton well, featuring the town's coaching inn The White Lion in his novel 'Tom Jones'. In a back room of the same establishment, the renowned Mrs Siddons gave a memorable acting performance.

UPTON-ON-SEVERN, THE BRIDGE 1931 84659

In Upton's churchyard lies a landlord of The White Lion. His epitaph reads: 'Here lies the landlord of the Lion, Who died in lively hopes of Zion; His son keeps on the business still, Resigned unto the heavenly will'.

UPTON-ON-SEVERN, THE RIVERSIDE 1931 84663

Dr John Dee held the living of Upton from 1553 until his death in 1608. A brilliant mathematician and scientist, Dee gained notoriety as an astrologer and sorcerer, being accused of trying to assassinate Elizabeth I. Dee died a sad and lonely genius, isolated from the Royal Court that had once given him such a warm welcome.

UPTON-ON-SEVERN, HIGH STREET 1931 84660A

In the days of Leland, that well-travelled topographer, the Severn was tidal at this point and large vessels reached the bridge at Upton; the bridge was the only crossing point on the river, apart from boats, between Gloucester and Worcester.

UPTON-ON-SEVERN, VIEW DOWN RIVER c1955 U12001

As with so many Severnside towns, Upton became popular with the boating fraternity during the 20th century. One of the very best ways to explore Worcestershire is to journey along its rivers.

WORCESTER, FRIAR STREET 1891 29321

The Cathedral city of Worcester is situated almost in the centre of Worcestershire, on the banks of the River Severn. Worcester developed as a settlement in Saxon times, though it did not achieve importance as a city until after the Norman Conquest.

WORCESTER, OLD HOUSE IN CORNMARKET c1890 W141508

Worcester is a city of elegant buildings, though a number were lost in the 20th century. But many more were restored and preserved so that we might enjoy them today. Mr Charles Collins, a Victorian builder, had his offices in this house in the Cornmarket.

WORCESTER, THE CATHEDRAL FROM THE SOUTH WEST 1891 29298

Work started on the present Worcester Cathedral in 1084. In the chancel, just before the high altar, is the tomb of King John, situated between the shrines of St Oswald and St Wulfstan. King John was particularly fond of Worcester, and was buried in the Cathedral at his own request. His tomb bears the first sculptured royal effigy in England, and is supposed to be a good likeness of the king.

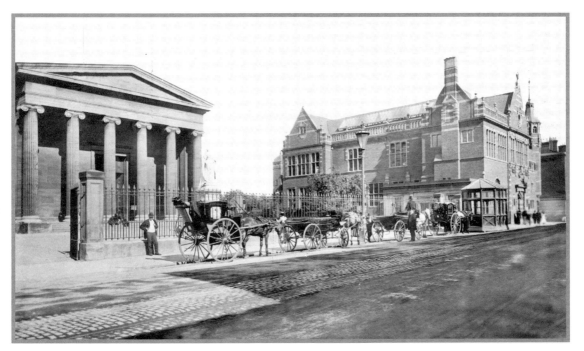

WORCESTER, THE SHIRE HALL AND THE INSTITUTE 1899 44008

The Victoria Institute contains Worcester's museum, art gallery and library and was built as a celebration of the Queen's Diamond Jubilee. Victoria's statue stands outside the columned Shire Hall next door.

WORCESTER
The Cross 1899 44010
The street known as The Cross continues from
Worcester's High Street. It was here that Elizabeth I
was greeted as she entered the city in 1574. The Cross
is dominated by the tower of St Nicholas's Church -
said to have been originally designed for St Martin's-
in-the-Fields in London.

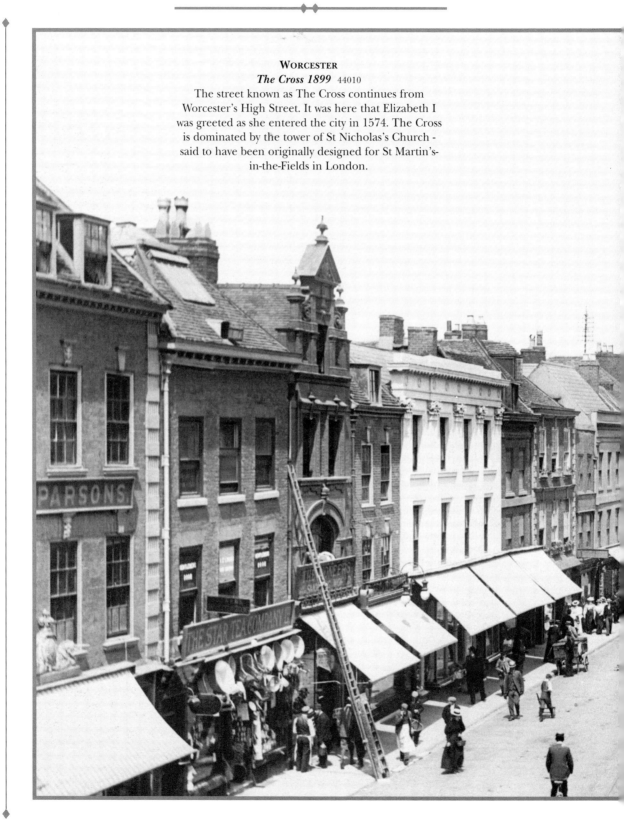

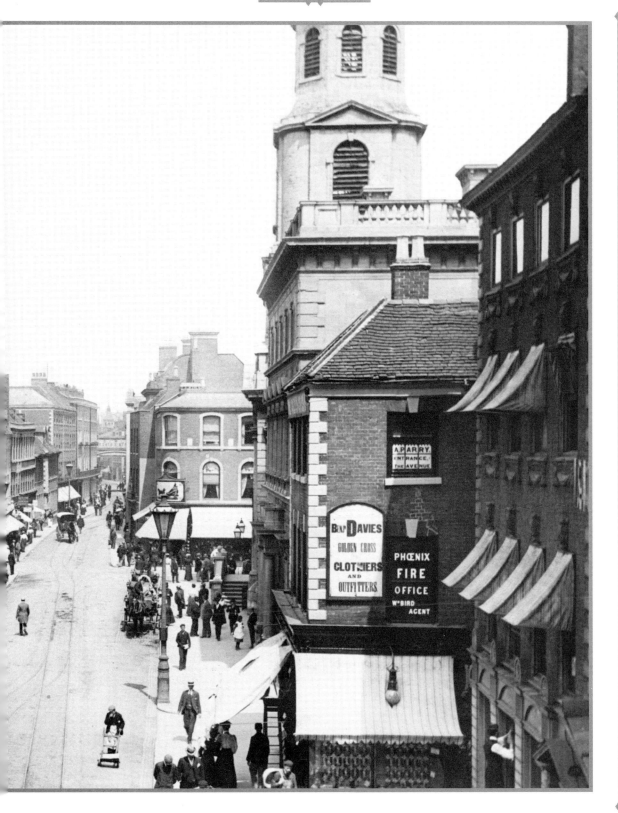

WORCESTER, THE CROSS 1896 38931
At the time of Leland, Worcester was a busy centre for the cloth trade. That careful observer tells us that 'the welthe of the towne standith most by draping, and noe towne of England at this present tyme maketh so many cloathes yearly as this towne doth'.

WORCESTER, THE GUILDHALL AND HIGH STREET 1904 51850

On the west side of the High Street stands the impressive frontage of Worcester's Guildhall. Designed by Thomas White, a local man thought to be a friend and student of Sir Christopher Wren, the Guildhall has statues of Charles I and II and the inscription 'May the Faithful City Flourish'. Above the doorway is a statue of Queen Anne, and nearby is a carved head of Oliver Cromwell, nailed to the building by the ears.

WORCESTER, KEPAX FERRY 1906 54272

Worcester has always had a very close relationship with the River Severn, from early times when the first community grew up around an ancient ford. There are many delightful walks along the banks of the Severn, and opportunities to take to the water in a variety of boats.

WORCESTER, THE CROSS 1923 73755

Worcester was a walled city until the 18th century, and witnessed a great deal of conflict, particularly during the English Civil War. Worcester's Cathedral has many monuments to warriors from all periods of history, including the men of the Worcestershire Regiment who fell in 'the three glorious victories on the banks of the Sutlej in 1845 and 1846'.

WORCESTER, THE CROSS 1923 73756

There have always been strong links between Worcester and royalty. Henry II and Eleanor of Aquitaine were crowned in the Cathedral, King John is buried there and his son Henry III came in great state for the re-dedication of the building. Edward I held a parliament in Worcester, and Prince Arthur, elder brother of Henry VIII, lies in the Cathedral.

WYRE PIDDLE, THE RIVER AVON c1955 W312001

This is a scene that might have been familiar to Worcestershire's earliest residents, for Wyre Piddle's church was built on the site of a prehistoric burial ground. It is quite probable that ancient dwellers crossed the Avon at a nearby ford and cultivated crops on the river's fertile flood plains.

WYRE PIDDLE, THE VILLAGE c1955 W312004

Wyre Piddle's church was built in 1888, though some of the original Norman building remains. The font is 12th-century, and there are some good examples of 15th-century glass. Wyre Piddle increased in size considerably during the 20th century.

WYRE PIDDLE, THE VILLAGE AND THE CROSS c1965 W312005

WYRE PIDDLE
The Village and the Cross c1965
This reconstructed wayside cross stands on the old highway between Worcester and Evesham. Only the steps, base and shaft of the original remains, the rest having been destroyed at some time in history.

WYRE PIDDLE
The Anchor c1965
So many towns and villages in Worcestershire are beautifully set on the banks of the county's rivers - as Wyre Piddle is on the Avon. It is an unforgettable experience to follow Worcestershire's rivers on foot or on a slow-moving boat.

WYRE PIDDLE, THE ANCHOR c1965 W312009

Index

Abberley 17, 18

Belbroughton 19

Beoley 24

Bewdley 20-21, 22, 23, 24

Bransford 25

Bredon 25, 26

Broadwas 26, 27

Broadway 27, 28

Bromsgrove 29, 30-31, 32

Bushley 32, 33

Castle Morton 33, 34

Chaddesley Corbett 35, 36

Churchill 36

Clifton upon Teme 37

Cropthorne 37, 38

Droitwich 39, 40-41

Elmley Castle 42

Evesham 43, 44-45, 46, 47, 48-49, 50

Feckenham 51, 52

Fladbury 52, 53

Great Comberton 53

Great Malvern 54, 55, 56, 57, 60

Great Witley 60, 61

Hallow 62, 63

Hanbury 63, 64

Hartlebury 64, 65

Holt Fleet 65, 66

Kempsey 66, 67, 68

Kidderminster 69, 70, 71

Kings Norton 72

Little Comberton 73, 74

Malvern Wells 57, 58-59

Longdon 75

Moseley 76

North Littleton 76

Ombersley 77

Pershore 78, 79, 80

Powick 80, 81, 82

Redditch 82, 83

Ribbesford 83, 84

Shrawley 84

South Littleton 85

Stanford Bridge 85, 86, 87

Stourbridge 88–89, 90

Stoke Prior 90

Stourport-on-Severn 91, 92, 93

Tenbury Wells 94, 95, 96-97, 98, 99, 100

Tibberton 101, 102

Upton-on-Severn 102, 103, 104, 105

Worcester 105, 106, 107, 108-109, 110, 111, 112

Wyre Piddle 113, 114

Frith Book Co Titles

Frith Book Company publish over 100 new titles each year. For latest catalogue please contact Frith Book Co.

Town Books 96pp, 100 photos. County and Themed Books 128pp, 150 photos (unless specified) All titles hardback laminated case and jacket except those indicated pb (paperback)

Around Bakewell	1-85937-113-2	£12.99
Around Barnstaple	1-85937-084-5	£12.99
Around Bath	1-85937-097-7	£12.99
Around Blackpool	1-85937-049-7	£12.99
Around Bognor Regis	1-85937-055-1	£12.99
Around Bournemouth	1-85937-067-5	£12.99
Around Bristol	1-85937-050-0	£12.99
British Life A Century Ago	1-85937-103-5	£17.99
Around Cambridge	1-85937-092-6	£12.99
Cambridgeshire	1-85937-086-1	£14.99
Cheshire	1-85937-045-4	£14.99
Around Chester	1-85937-090-X	£12.99
Around Chesterfield	1-85937-071-3	£12.99
Around Chichester	1-85937-089-6	£12.99
Cornwall	1-85937-054-3	£14.99
Cotswolds	1-85937-099-3	£14.99
Cumbria	1-85937-101-9	£14.99
Around Derby	1-85937-046-2	£12.99
Devon	1-85937-052-7	£14.99
Dorset	1-85937-075-6	£14.99
Dorset Coast	1-85937-062-4	£14.99
Down the Thames	1-85937-121-3	£14.99
Around Dublin	1-85937-058-6	£12.99
East Anglia	1-85937-059-4	£14.99
Around Eastbourne	1-85937-061-6	£12.99
English Castles	1-85937-078-0	£14.99
Essex	1-85937-082-9	£14.99
Around Exeter	1-85937-126-4	£12.99
Around Falmouth	1-85937-066-7	£12.99
Around Great Yarmouth	1-85937-085-3	£12.99
Greater Manchester	1-85937-108-6	£14.99
Hampshire	1-85937-064-0	£14.99
Around Harrogate	1-85937-112-4	£12.99
Hertfordshire	1-85937-079-9	£14.99

Isle of Man	1-85937-065-9	£14.99
Isle of Wight	1-85937-114-0	£14.99
Around Leicester	1-85937-073-x	£12.99
Around Lincoln	1-85937-111-6	£12.99
Around Liverpool	1-85937-051-9	£12.99
Around Maidstone	1-85937-056-X	£12.99
North Yorkshire	1-85937-048-9	£14.99
Northumberland and Tyne & Wear		
	1-85937-072-1	£14.99
Around Nottingham	1-85937-060-8	£12.99
Around Oxford	1-85937-096-9	£12.99
Oxfordshire	1-85937-076-4	£14.99
Around Penzance	1-85937-069-1	£12.99
Around Plymouth	1-85937-119-1	£12.99
Around Reading	1-85937-087-X	£12.99
Around St Ives	1-85937-068-3	£12.99
Around Salisbury	1-85937-091-8	£12.99
Around Scarborough	1-85937-104-3	£12.99
Scottish Castles	1-85937-077-2	£14.99
Around Sevenoaks and Tonbridge		
	1-85937-057-8	£12.99
Sheffield and S Yorkshire	1-85937-070-5	£14.99
Around Southport	1-85937-106-x	£12.99
Around Shrewsbury	1-85937-110-8	£12.99
Shropshire	1-85937-083-7	£14.99
South Devon Coast	1-85937-107-8	£14.99
Staffordshire (96pp)	1-85937-047-0	£12.99
Around Stratford upon Avon		
	1-85937-098-5	£12.99
Suffolk	1-85937-074-8	£14.99
Surrey	1-85937-081-0	£14.99
Around Torbay	1-85937-063-2	£12.99
Welsh Castles	1-85937-120-5	£14.99
West Midlands	1-85937-109-4	£14.99
Wiltshire	1-85937-053-5	£14.99

Frith Book Co Titles Available in 2000

Canals and Waterways	1-85937-129-9	£17.99	Apr
Around Guildford	1-85937-117-5	£12.99	Apr
Around Horsham	1-85937-127-2	£12.99	Apr
Around Ipswich	1-85937-133-7	£12.99	Apr
Ireland (pb)	1-85937-181-7	£9.99	Apr
London (pb)	1-85937-183-3	£9.99	Apr
New Forest	1-85937-128-0	£14.99	Apr
Around Newark	1-85937-105-1	£12.99	Apr
Around Newquay	1-85937-140-x	£12.99	Apr
Scotland (pb)	1-85937-182-5	£9.99	Apr
Around Southampton	1-85937-088-8	£12.99	Apr
Sussex (pb)	1-85937-184-1	£9.99	Apr
Around Winchester	1-85937-139-6	£12.99	Apr
Around Belfast	1-85937-094-2	£12.99	May
Colchester (pb)	1-85937-188-4	£8.99	May
Dartmoor	1-85937-145-0	£14.99	May
Exmoor	1-85937-132-9	£14.99	May
Leicestershire (pb)	1-85937-185-x	£9.99	May
Lincolnshire	1-85937-135-3	£14.99	May
North Devon Coast	1-85937-146-9	£14.99	May
Nottinghamshire (pb)	1-85937-187-6	£9.99	May
Peak District	1-85937-100-0	£14.99	May
Redhill to Reigate	1-85937-137-x	£12.99	May
Around Truro	1-85937-147-7	£12.99	May
Yorkshire (pb)	1-85937-186-8	£9.99	May
Berkshire (pb)	1-85937-191-4	£9.99	Jun
Brighton (pb)	1-85937-192-2	£8.99	Jun
Churches of Berkshire	1-85937-170-1	£17.99	Jun
Churches of Dorset	1-85937-172-8	£17.99	Jun
Derbyshire (pb)	1-85937-196-5	£9.99	Jun
East Sussex	1-85937-130-2	£14.99	Jun
Edinburgh (pb)	1-85937-193-0	£8.99	Jun
Norwich (pb)	1-85937-194-9	£8.99	Jun
South Devon Living Memories			
	1-85937-168-x	£14.99	Jun

Stone Circles & Ancient Monuments			
	1-85937-143-4	£17.99	Jun
Victorian & Edwardian Kent			
	1-85937-149-3	£14.99	Jun
Warwickshire (pb)	1-85937-203-1	£9.99	Jun
Buckinghamshire (pb)	1-85937-200-7	£9.99	Jul
Down the Severn	1-85937-118-3	£14.99	Jul
Kent (pb)	1-85937-189-2	£9.99	Jul
Victorian & Edwardian Yorkshire			
	1-85937-154-x	£14.99	Jul
West Sussex	1-85937-148-5	£14.99	Jul
Cornish Coast	1-85937-163-9	£14.99	Aug
County Durham	1-85937-123-x	£14.99	Aug
Croydon Living Memories	1-85937-162-0	£12.99	Aug
Dorset Living Memories	1-85937-210-4	£14.99	Aug
Glasgow (pb)	1-85937-190-6	£8.99	Aug
Gloucestershire	1-85937-102-7	£14.99	Aug
Herefordshire	1-85937-174-4	£14.99	Aug
Kent Living Memories	1-85937-125-6	£14.99	Aug
Lancashire (pb)	1-85937-197-3	£9.99	Aug
Manchester (pb)	1-85937-198-1	£8.99	Aug
North London	1-85937-206-6	£14.99	Aug
Somerset	1-85937-153-1	£14.99	Aug
Tees Valley & Cleveland	1-85937-211-2	£14.99	Aug
Worcestershire	1-85937-152-3	£14.99	Aug
Victorian & Edwardian Maritime Album			
	1-85937-144-2	£17.99	Aug

Available from your local bookshop or from the publisher

FRITH PRODUCTS & SERVICES

Francis Frith would doubtless be pleased to know that the pioneering publishing venture he started in 1860 still continues today. More than a hundred and thirty years later, The Francis Frith Collection continues in the same innovative tradition and is now one of the foremost publishers of vintage photographs in the world. Some of the current activities include:

Interior Decoration

Today Frith's photographs can be seen framed and as giant wall murals in thousands of pubs, restaurants, hotels, banks, retail stores and other public buildings throughout the country. In every case they enhance the unique local atmosphere of the places they depict and provide reminders of gentler days in an increasingly busy and frenetic world.

Product Promotions

Frith products have been used by many major companies to promote the sales of their own products or to reinforce their own history and heritage. Brands include Hovis bread, Courage beers, Scots Porage Oats, Colman's mustard, Cadbury's foods, Mellow Birds coffee, Dunhill pipe tobacco, Guinness, and Bulmer's Cider.

Genealogy and Family History

As the interest in family history and roots grows world-wide, more and more people are turning to Frith's photographs of Great Britain for images of the towns, villages and streets where their ancestors lived; and, of course, photographs of the churches and chapels where their ancestors were christened, married and buried are an essential part of every genealogy tree and family album.
A series of easy-to-use CD Roms is planned for publication, and an increasing number of Frith photographs will be able to be viewed on specialist genealogy sites. A growing range of Frith books will be available on CD.

Frith Products

All Frith photographs are available Framed or just as Mounted Prints, and can be ordered from the address below. From time to time other products - Address Books, Calendars, Table Mats, etc - are available.

The Internet

Already thousands of Frith photographs can be viewed and purchased on the internet. By the end of the year 2000 some 60,000 Frith photographs will be available on the internet. The number of sites is constantly expanding, each focussing on different products and services from the Collection.
Some of the sites are listed below.

www.townpages.co.uk
www.icollector.com
www.barclaysquare.co.uk
www.cornwall-online.co.uk

For more detailed information on Frith companies and products, look at these sites:
www.francisfrith.co.uk
www.frithbook.co.uk
www.francisfrith.com

See the complete list of Frith Books at:

www.frithbook.co.uk

This web site is regularly updated with the latest list of publications from the Frith Book Company Ltd. If you wish to buy books relating to another part of the country that your local bookshop does not stock, you may purchase on-line.

For further information, trade, or author enquiries please contact us at the address below:
The Francis Frith Collection, Frith's Barn, Teffont, Salisbury, Wiltshire, England SP3 5QP.
Tel: +44 (0)1722 716 376 Fax: +44 (0)1722 716 881 Email: uksales@francisfrith.com

To receive your FREE Mounted Print

Mounted Print
Overall size 14 x 11 inches

Cut out this Voucher and return it with your remittance for £1.50 to cover postage and handling.
Choose any photograph included in this book. Your SEPIA print will be A4 in size, and mounted in a cream mount with burgundy rule lines, overall size 14 x 11 inches.

Order additional Mounted Prints at HALF PRICE (only £7.49 each*)

If there are further pictures you would like to order, possibly as gifts for friends and family, acquire them at half price (no additional postage and handling required).

Have your Mounted Prints framed*

For an additional £14.95 per print you can have your chosen Mounted Print framed in an elegant polished wood and gilt moulding, overall size 16 x 13 inches (no additional postage and handling required).

---

* IMPORTANT!
These special prices are only available if ordered using the original voucher on this page (no copies permitted) and at the same time as your free Mounted Print, for delivery to the same address

---

Frith Collectors' Guild

From time to time we publish a magazine of news and stories about Frith photographs and further special offers of Frith products. If you would like 12 months FREE membership, please return this form.

Send completed forms to:
**The Francis Frith Collection,
Frith's Barn, Teffont, Salisbury,
Wiltshire SP3 5QP**

Voucher for FREE and Reduced Price Frith Prints

Picture no.	Page number	Qty	Mounted @ £7.49	Framed + £14.95	Total Cost
		1	**Free of charge***	£	£
			£7.49	£	£
			£7.49	£	£
			£7.49	£	£
			£7.49	£	£
			£7.49	£	£

Please allow 28 days for delivery	* Post & handling	£1.50
Book Title	**Total Order Cost**	£

Please do not photocopy this voucher. Only the original is valid, so please cut it out and return it to us.

I enclose a cheque / postal order for £ . . . .
made payable to 'The Francis Frith Collection'
OR please debit my Mastercard / Visa / Switch / Amex card

Number . . . .

Expires . . . . Signature . . . .

Name Mr/Mrs/Ms . . . .

Address . . . .

. . . .

. . . .

. . . . Postcode . . . .

Daytime Tel No . . . .   Valid to 31/12/01

The Francis Frith Collectors' Guild

Please enrol me as a member for 12 months free of charge.

Name Mr/Mrs/Ms . . . .

Address . . . .

. . . .

. . . .

. . . . Postcode . . . .

Free Print - see overleaf